L.A.DECO

L.A. Deco

CARLA BREEZE Introduction by David Gebhard

Rizzoli
NEW YORK

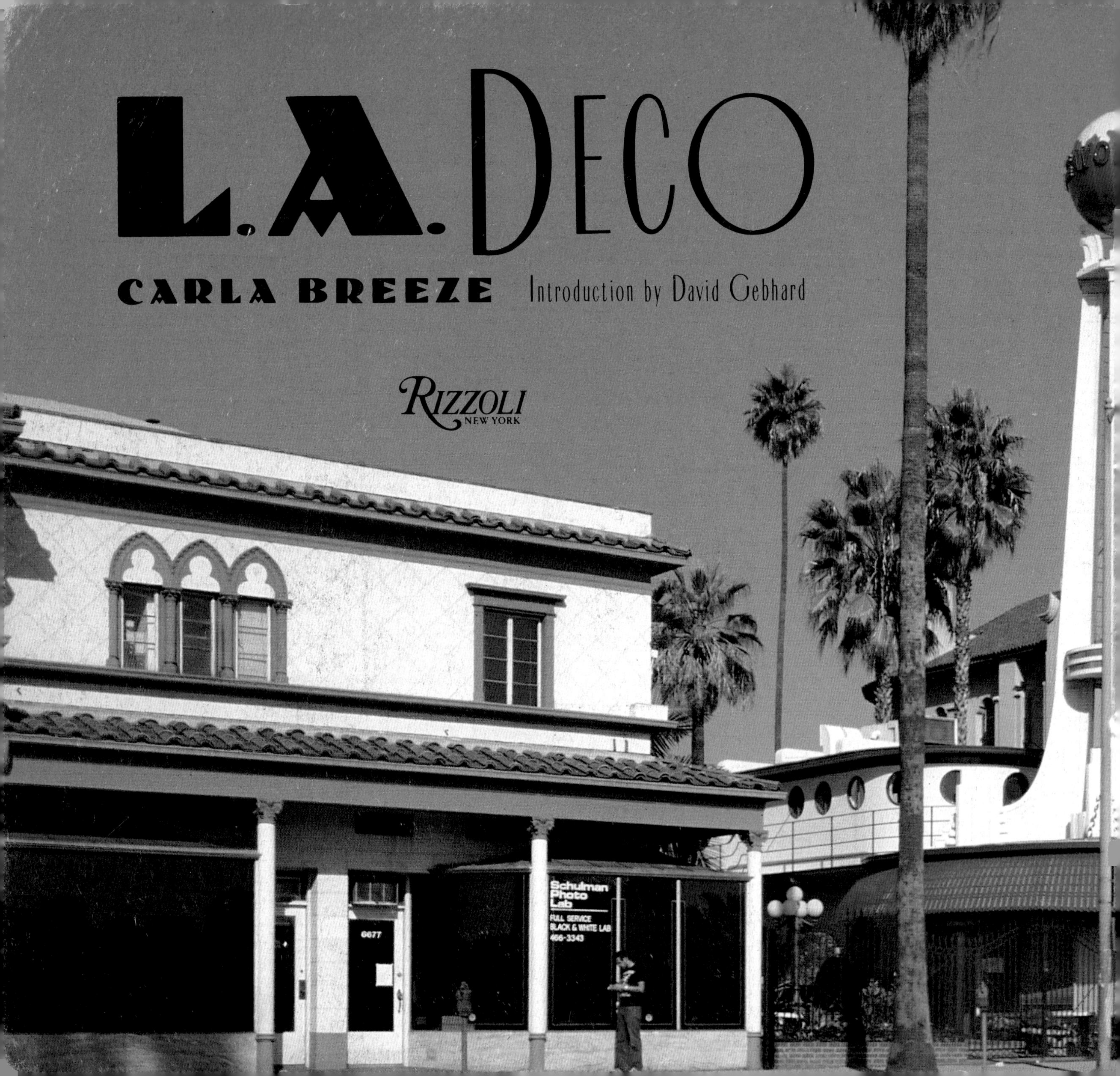

Schulman
Photo
Lab

FULL SERVICE
BLACK & WHITE LAB
466-3343

6677

ACKNOWLEDGMENTS
▼

The following individuals have all contributed to the realization of this book: David Gebhard, whose extensive research and publications have been relied upon, especially *Architecture in Los Angeles: A Compleat Guide* with Robert Winter and *L.A. in the Thirties* with Harriette von Breton; Robert Janjigian, my editor at Rizzoli International Publications; Ernst Wilde of Victor Hasselbad, Inc., who supplied the Superwide/M camera used for this project; Maureen Sugden; Gary Selden; Merle O'Keeffe; Joyce Gibson; Wayne Decker; Marvin Steputis; Carolyn Malone; Robert Kramer; Bernice Thomas; Mona and Walter Lutz; Julius and Ossie Decker; Marcia Decker; Nick Schutz Decker, Janet Sternberg and Dr. Steven Lavine; Janice Brooks; Toby Moss of the Toby Moss Gallery; Carol and Michael Daugherty, owners of the Lloyd Wright-designed Derby house, which they have carefully and respectfully restored; Joe Caliva, Neva Jennings, Rocky Westlake, and

William Delbert of the South Catalina Island Company; Lisa Gotori of the Oviatt Building; Rena Wasserman and Candy Croteau of the Wiltern Theater; Laurie Davenport and Marie Ortega of I. Magnin, the current owner of the Bullock's Wilshire store; Dr. Carol Soucek King, editor in chief of *Designers West*; Charles C. Bricker, Jr; David Roth of Premiere, owner of the Banks-Huntly Building; Susan Tunick; Dennis Daze of Transcon Property Services, Inc., owner of the Garfield Building; Howard Morhaim, my agent; Felix Cordero; and D.M. Carlick.

CARLA BREEZE

LEFT
Detail, small tower above a circa 1931 retail store at the corner of 43rd Place and Degnan Avenue in the Leimert Park shopping district.

OPPOSITE
A magnificent marquee hangs above the entrance to the Pantages Theater, built in 1929 by architect B. Marcus Priteca. It is located at 6233 Hollywood Blvd.

Los Angeles and the Art Deco

by David Gebhard

The verbal and written affair of discussing the arts in terms of this or that style provides a fascinating history in its own right, irrespective of the visual objects being categorized. The term Art Deco is no exception. During the years when Art Deco as a style was in fashion, the term itself was essentially unknown, with "Modernistic" and "Style Moderne" used instead. The term Art Deco was coined many years later, in 1968, by the British critic and historian Bevis Hillier. As one would expect, the invention of this term has more to do with the market for decorative art in the late 1960s than it does with the twenties or thirties.[1]

The term quickly caught on, in part due to its obvious references to the 1925 Paris Exposition International des Arts Décoratifs et Industriels Modernes and to Art Nouveau, the earlier but brief stylistic episode popular at the turn of the century. By the early 1970s, the term Art Deco was in widespread use and today it is broadly accepted, with its meaning continually expanded.

While this expansion has diluted the term, it has encouraged a reassessment of design made in the teens, twenties, and thirties. Now we can see more clearly the similarity between the abstraction of outwardly historic forms and the specific context of abstract designs considered to be "popular" or "High Art Modern." However one views the expansion of visual motifs and forms now gathered within the fold of Art Deco, it is important to remember that style terms do have their own lives and our task is simply to follow along and be aware of their changing nuances.

In the early 1930s, just before the effects of the Great Depression were fully felt, American architects intensely debated the pros and cons of modernism versus traditionalism.[2] The 1920s had witnessed not only the emergence of a new puritanical International Style Modernism, but also a popular modernism that would come to be known as Art Deco (based to a considerable extent upon work previewed at the famed 1925 Paris exposition). This decade also represented a high point in the application of traditional (and not so traditional) historic imagery to a wide variety of old and new building types.

The ideological battleground between modernist and traditionalist schools was complicated by the existence of the popular Art Deco style. Here was a set of modernist images that was both "smart" and modern, and at the same time highly traditional, its architectural language easily maneuvered into many of the traditional historic decorative schemes.

American architects dug into the past and produced Art Deco buildings inspired by Classical, Gothic, Beaux-Arts, and Pre-Columbian styles of Mexico and Central America as well as by the Indian and Spanish adobe pueblos of the American Southwest. American designers of these Art Deco buildings were inspired by the classical training they had received at the Ecole des Beaux-Arts in Paris (and designs emanating from Paris were always considered the most correct and fashionable).

From its inception in the early 1920s, Art Deco

had been seen essentially as an urban style. It is not surprising that New York, Chicago, and San Francisco should quickly emerge as Art Deco centers. What was unusual was that Los Angeles should also emerge as a prominent center. The reasons why, in part, are the same as those that account for the city's rapid rise to preeminence within all the architectural styles employed in that decade.[3]

To many Americans, Los Angeles has always assumed a mythical dimension—an Arcadia transformed into reality. The city's mild climate, the illusion of perpetual sunshine, the varied natural backdrop, with snow-covered mountains to the east and vast expanses of sandy ocean beaches to the west—all implied a healthy, hygienic, and "good" life. To this remote coastal Arcadia came thousands of migrants, including a growing number of sophisticated and wealthy patrons as well as a contingent of architects and designers to satisfy their needs.

The illusion of a misty Arcadia loomed large in the eyes of a number of European modernists who found themselves in a dismal social, political, and economic climate after World War I. In moving to Southern California, these architects brought with them the modernism of early 1900s Vienna, Darmstadt, and Berlin and they applied these lessons not only to architecture and design but also to the emerging Hollywood film industry and its stage sets. In addition, a highly diverse group of American architects, ranging from the "native" avant-gardists Frank Lloyd Wright, his eldest son Lloyd, Bruce Goff, and Barry Byrne to Beaux-Arts-trained Stiles Clements (of Morgan,

9

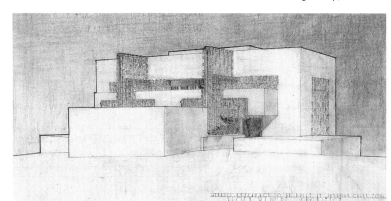

Walls, Clements) and the "way-out" Mayan revivalist Robert B. Stacy-Judd, also influenced the evolution of the Art Deco style. These architects played a variety of games with their images, ranging from a suggestion of international and national connections to strong statements of regionalism.

Since Art Deco was essentially decorative, it could be easily incorporated within such existing styles as Classical, Beaux-Arts, or Pre-Columbian. On some occasions, the design was intended to be read as an avowed expression of the modern (or the moderne), as was the case at the Bullock's Wilshire Department Store (1928; Parkinson and Parkinson, Feil and Paradice, and Jock Peters). In other instances, such as the Mausoleum of the Golden West (1927; Ross Montgomery), Art Deco was used to update and enliven the Classical or Baroque tradition.

The Art Deco approach to ornament is present in many of the Spanish Colonial revival designs of Morgan, Walls, Clements, as well as in the Los Angeles work of Frank Lloyd Wright and son Lloyd Wright. There was even a brief period in the mid-1920s when R.M. Schindler, one of America's principal exponents of the High Art Modern, turned to the language of the Art Deco for modest single- and multiple-family housing.[4] Concrete was the favored material of these Los Angeles architects—used in reinforced-concrete walls that revealed a pattern of form boards, concrete block, or cast concrete. With the slightest twist in design, even cement-stucco-sheathed walls nominally associated with Mediterranean and Spanish Colonial revival styles could be made to read as Art Deco.

The International Art Deco did draw from the exotic vocabulary of Pre-Columbian architecture. But from 1910 on, it was in California (and especially in Southern California) that an attempt was made to transform these non-European themes into a new regional language. Frank Lloyd Wright, for example, used Pre-Columbian motifs in several of his early Midwestern designs. But it was in his 1917–1920 Barnsdall house on Olive Hill as well as in his later pre-cast concrete- block houses built in the mid-1920s that he combined Pre-Columbian, Southwestern Pueblo, and Art Deco to produce what he described as a new organic regionalism for California and the Southwest.[5] His son, Lloyd Wright, participated as an architect and landscape architect in this new regionalism in such designs as the Samuel-Navarro house of 1926–1928, and the sense of modernity via Art Deco was heightened even more.[6] Finally, it was a transplanted English architect, Robert B. Stacy-Judd, who turned the vocabulary of the Pre-Columbian style into something of a Los Angeles cult (similar in spirit to the religious and social cults that have flourished in Southern California since the late nineteenth century). His 1931 First Baptist Church in Ventura (just north of Los Angeles) presents the unbelievable marriage of Pre-Columbian and Art Deco styles with such hybrid details as an Aztec sacrificial altar transformed into a pulpit.

Though Los Angeles is considered a horizontal city, it also has been home to the favorite building type of the Art Deco period, the skyscraper. By the opening years of the 1930s, Los Angeles could boast several preeminent skyscrapers, among them the 1928 black and gold-sheathed Richfield building (1928; Morgan, Walls, Clements, now destroyed), the green and gold-Eastern Building (1929; Claude Beelman), and

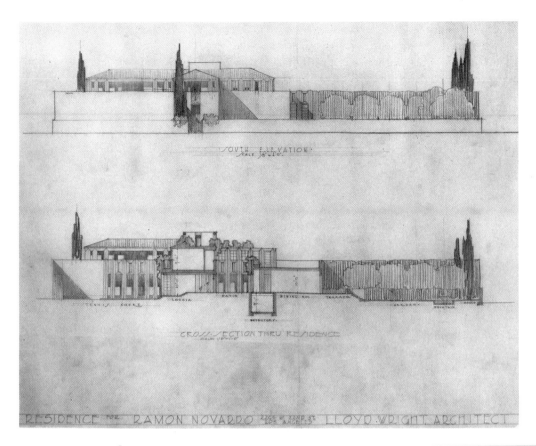

RESIDENCE for RAMON NOVARRO 2262 W. 22ND ST.
LLOYD WRIGHT ARCHITECT

Cross-section and south elevation, Samuel-
Navarro residence, 2262 West 22nd Street,
Los Angeles, 1926–1928, Lloyd Wright.
Courtesy of Architectural Drawing Collection,
University Art Museum, University of
California, Santa Barbara.

RIGHT
Sketch (1928), First Baptist Church, Ventura,
California, 1931, Robert B. Stacy-Judd.
Courtesy of Architectural Drawing Collection,
University Art Museum, University of
California, Santa Barbara.

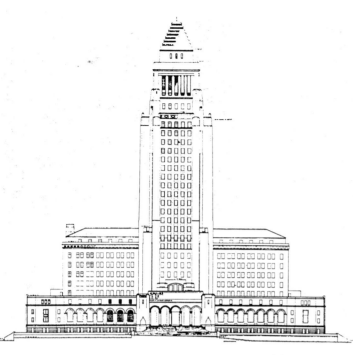

ABOVE
West elevation, Los Angeles City Hall, Temple and Main Streets, Downtown Los Angeles, 1926–1928, John C. Austin, Parkinson and Parkinson, Albert C. Martin, and Austin Whittlesey.

RIGHT
Detail, upper portion of tower, Los Angeles City Hall.

the most sophisticated of them all, the Bullock's Wilshire store.

By the early 1930s, the city's system of east/west boulevards, extending from Downtown Los Angeles to the Pacific ocean, was dotted with occasional skyscrapers, small Art Deco stores and office buildings, motion picture theaters, drive-in markets, garages, and service stations. Wilshire Boulevard's Miracle Mile, with its implications of the linear city, displayed a number of small skyscrapers, such as the ten-story Dominguez-Wilshire Building (1930; Morgan, Walls, Clements).

The style was also frequently used for governmental buildings. Los Angeles City Hall (1926–28; John C. Austin, Parkinson and Parkinson, Albert C. Martin and Austin Whittlesey) was a skyscraper set, like Bertram G. Goodhue's earlier Nebraska State Capitol Building, on a classically designed base. The shaft of the Los Angeles City Hall recalled both the Hellenistic world of the Mausoleum of Halicarnassus and the massing, patterning, and decorative sensibility associated with Art Deco.

By the end of the twenties, Los Angeles could boast many Art Deco-style buildings. There were strip and suburban low-rise office buildings, shopping centers, manufacturing plants, and warehouses. As was true in other parts of the country, the Art Deco style was also used in a purely sculptural mode for grave markers and mausoleums. While there were a good number of splendid Art

Deco apartment houses built in Los Angeles during these years, such as Sunset Tower in Hollywood (1929–31; Leland A. Bryant), there were only a handful of single-family houses designed in this style.

Popular Moderne had to be transformed into the next phase of Streamlined Moderne before modernity had a widespread impact on middle-class and upper-middle-class, single-family dwellings. Though few in number, Los Angeles's Art Deco single-family houses represent major contributions to the style. The 1929–30 West Los Angeles house of Nelson K. Smith (1929–30; J.C. Smale) is one of the few examples of formal Art Deco monumentality applied to a building. Indicative of the strong connections between Europe and the West Coast is the Santa Monica Canyon house of Hollywood scenic designer Cedric Gibbons (1929; Cedric Gibbons and Douglas Honnold): it offers a fascinating play of Art Deco and International Style imagery.

William Lingenbrink, a unique figure within the Los Angeles scene of the twenties and thirties, became a passionate convert to modernism, com-

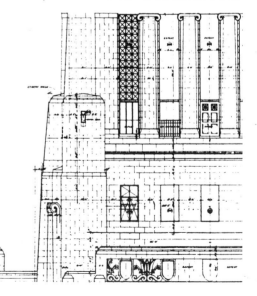

missioning various architects to design Art Deco and International Style commercial and residential buildings. He also published books on the subject (among them, *Modernistic Architecture*, Los Angeles, 1933). Another of Lingenbrink's unusual contributions was the establishment of the San Fernando Valley community of Park Moderne. Here Jock Peters, Schindler, and others designed houses that illustrated how an entire small village could go modern.

During the Depression, Art Deco buildings continued to rise in Los Angeles—primarily in a style we now call P.W.A. Moderne.[7] These stripped classical buildings employ vertical articulated surfaces accompanied by a sparse usage of Art Deco ornamental motifs such as spirals, zigzags, and triangles. Buildings, such as the Federal Building and Post Office (1938–1940, Louis A. Simmons, Gilbert Stanley Underwood), through the simplifying of surfaces, elimination of entabla-

ture and cornices, and an increased emphasis on rectilinear volumes, became modern.

Many of these late P.W.A. Moderne Art Deco buildings absorbed motifs from the then newly fashionable Streamline Moderne. Curved and rounded surfaces and banding, walls of glass bricks, and other elements of the Streamline Moderne entered into these designs. Though World War II is generally considered as a signal of the end of both Art Deco and Streamline Moderne, such was not the case in Los Angeles or elsewhere throughout the country. In the decade after 1945, a significant number of Art Deco-style structures were built in Los Angeles. In these late designs, ornament was eliminated but other Art Deco motifs were very much in evidence.

To fully capture Los Angeles's involvement with Art Deco, one should experience the buildings' interiors as well as their furniture (especially that designed by Kem Weber and Jock Peters). Above all, the spirit of Art Deco was captured in the stage sets made for so many Hollywood movies from the 1920s and 1930s. Within these artifacts, the mythical as well as the actual atmosphere of Los Angeles lives on.

13

CHAPTER ONE

Theaters and Entertainment

Theaters have been integral to the history of California. The madness of the 1849 Gold Rush induced an equally frantic lust for dance halls, vaudeville, and entertainment in any form. Lola Montez, a vaudeville actress, performed a spider dance that dazzled miners and millionaires. Lotta Crabtree, an eight-year-old performer managed by her mother, toured every flimsy mining camp in California.[1] By the end of the nineteenth century, legitimate theaters in Los Angeles were housed in expensively designed and executed edifices favoring revival styles redolent of luxury—Renaissance, Baroque, and Louis XVI.

As early as 1921, film brought modern architecture before the American public. In the sets for the movie *Enchantment*, architect Joseph Urban juxtaposed architectural elements against stylized floral wall patterns.[2] Urban, initially associated with the Viennese Secessionist movement in his native Austria, came to the United States in the early 1920s and began creating stage sets for theater and opera. Through Florenz Ziegfeld, owner of the famed Ziegfeld Follies and a primary client, Urban met William Randolph Hearst when the newspaper publisher was just forming the Cosmopolitan Productions company to showcase the talents of his lover, Marion Davies.[3] As art director of numerous movies for Cosmopolitan Productions, Urban merged Secessionist detail with modernist aesthetics.

This was not the first taste of Secessionism or modernism. During the late nineteenth and early

twentieth centuries, expositions had been the primary forum to introduce the latest developments in design, decoration, and technical innovations. Austria's pavilion at the 1904 St. Louis World's Fair featured Secessionist decorative arts in rooms designed by Joseph Urban.[4]

As movies became more acceptable, so did the theaters screening them and their design began to reflect their new status. "Recollection calls to mind the days when it was considered degrading to attend the so-called 'movie shows,'" wrote an architect in 1925.

How, after a careful survey up and down the street to make sure that no acquaintance was within sight, a nickel or dime was deposited with a lady in a showcase, and then with ticket in hand a hurried plunge was made through the entrance door into a dank,

mysterious and black interior! . . . At that time these palaces of dubious entertainment were usually buildings intended for other purposes and converted into public halls. Frequently the exteriors were adorned after the manner of a sideshow at the circus; and in the interiors the seats were arranged much as they would be in a slum mission, with flat floors and little or no ventilation.[5]

In 1916, D.W. Griffith, one of the first great American movie directors, erected a fabulous movie set for *Intolerance* on a bare lot at what is now 4473 Sunset Drive.[6] The set—a re-creation of the ancient city of Babylon—featured figures of elephants on hind legs atop massive grooved columns and square stepped arches. Left standing for several years, this semi-permanent structure instilled an obsession with ziggurats and prehistoric architecture.

LEFT
Stiles O. Clements of Morgan, Walls, Clements, one of the Los Angeles area's oldest architectural firms, designed the 1930–1931 Wiltern Theater/Pellissier Building complex at the corner of Western Avenue and Wilshire Blvd.

OPPOSITE
The Avalon Theater, in the 1929 Webber and Spaulding-designed Casino complex on Santa Catalina Island, features rainbow-hued murals painted by John Gabriel Beckman.

14

Movie mogul Sid Grauman hired the San Francisco architect William Lee Woollett to design his first major movie theater in Los Angeles, the Metropolitan Theater, in the early 1920s. By 1921, he turned to a Los Angeles firm, Meyer and Holler, to design the first "exotic" theater in Hollywood, Grauman's Egyptian Theater. This very successful and influential Art Deco theater was located at the end of a long forecourt lined with shops. Decorated with details derived from Old and New Kingdom art—bas reliefs (of incised cement to imitate limestone), murals, engaged columns, and stepped pyramids—the design of the Hollywood theater created a rage for Egyptian motifs. The style was soon applied to other American theaters, along with the Hollywood Cemetery and numerous Los Angeles apartment buildings. Encouraged by the success of the Egyptian Theater, Meyer and Holler were commissioned to design the world-famous Grauman's Chinese Theater.

With its jade-colored roofs, cinnabarlike terracotta surfaces, and gold ornamentation, Grauman's Chinese Theater became an instant success—especially after movie stars began leaving their handprints, footprints and signatures in the forecourt's cement (a shrewd publicity stunt that has attracted much attention to this day). Figures of dragons and other references to Chinese culture proliferate. Tickets for screenings could be purchased under an open temple structure. The pressure to produce an outstanding theater smack in the middle of movie-making territory is well stated in the following quote from G. Albert Lansburgh: "In designing this theater the problem was to plan a dramatic house that would have rather an exotic character, since the theater is in Hollywood, where a majority of the residents demand the extraordinary."[7]

Lansburgh made this statement regarding his work on another Los Angeles theater, El Capitan,

but it surely applied to any architectural endeavor in Hollywood during the 1920s.

The growing popularity and acceptance of theater design was recognized in the June 1925 issue of *Architectural Forum*: the entire issue was devoted to theater design, both stage and cinema. Subjects covered were technical (one article was titled "Some Structural Features of Theaters"), psychological, and aesthetic. In an article about theater entrances and lobbies, for example, readers were told that

. . . the lobby should be designed and so equipped that the fascination resulting from it will keep the patron's mind off the fact he is waiting . . . fine paintings, impressive statuary, costly rugs and beautiful tapestries, used for decoration, have a marked effect on the waiting patron.[8]

John Gabriel Beckman, the muralist and designer responsible for much of the interior of Grauman's Chinese Theater, also worked on the Avalon, an innovative theater located within the Casino complex on Santa Catalina Island, twenty-six miles off the coast of Los Angeles. At the Avalon, Beckman worked with architect Sumner A. Spaulding and his partner, Walter Webber, to produce a fanciful design that departed from the exotic trend by using underwater themes and California historical imagery.

The almost true hemispherical ceiling is dotted with stars against a midnight blue background. The surrounding walls are adorned with painted Indians racing on horseback, Franciscan monks, and Spanish galleons entwined with sinuous floral and water ripple motifs. Oriental faces form keystones over the exits.

Purely Art Deco, the Avalon Theater incorporates regional imagery and decorative motifs. The theater was designed specifically to screen movies with sound and its acoustics were so

successful that engineers working on Radio City Music Hall visited the structure to gain technical expertise.[9]

The Avalon Casino, designed by Webber and Spaulding was essentially a reinforced-steel barrel volume that featured a ballroom placed above the movie theater and a movable ticket cage to ensure even wear on the entrance pavilion's Catalina-tile floor. Placing the ballroom above the theater was not easy, as Webber recalled:

The desire for a dance hall as large as possible inspired the idea of a complete overhanging balcony 14 feet wide around the building at this level for circulation . . . . The theater auditorium, 138 feet wide, required a ceiling height of 43 feet. This raised the floor level of the ballroom 45 feet above the entrance level of the street. The problem of asking people to climb four or five stories was a trying one. Elevators did not seem practical for such large crowds. Then Mr. Wrigley himself suggested ramps like those used in his ball parks. These ramps . . . fit perfectly into the two corners of the triangular site left after the circular building was located.[10]

The Casino, widely regarded as an outstanding building, received an award from the Southern California Chapter of the American Institute of Architects in 1930.

By the early 1920s, the film industry had replaced oil, shipping, and agriculture as Los Angeles's leading industry.[11] To gain control over distribution, companies such as RKO, 20th Century Fox, and Warner Brothers began to lease or build movie theaters. By the late 1920s, issues of cost began to pervade theater design. (In 1925, theater construction cost anywhere from $125 to $200 per seat.) No wonder that the modernistic style with its geometric features, less expensive than other ornate decorative styles, was frequently selected for theater design. Now the patron

was to be "taken up on the architect's magic carpet, and set down suddenly in a celestial city of gorgeous stage settings, luxurious hangings, and enchanting music"—but this would have to be accomplished within a budget.[12] Escapism had always been part of the enjoyment of movies; theaters located in mining and factory towns and "tenement house districts" often had the fullest houses.[13] This called for escapist-oriented architecture and interior design.

Apparently lacking such patronage, Warner Brothers's Western Theater, now the Wiltern, closed after only one year in operation.[14] This fabulous concoction, the result of Stiles O. Clements's collaboration with G. Albert Lansburgh, the noted theater architect, exuded luxury; it was a magical realm adorned with sun and wave motifs and

tropical foliation reflective of the paradisiacal environment of Southern California. The sun appears in plaster relief on the marquee's ceiling, over the corbeled arches of the lobby, and on the auditorium's ceiling. The original furniture was designed by Kem Weber, a noted industrial designer of the time. Despite its initial short-lived success, the theater reopened in the mid-1930s and operated until 1979. Fortunately, the Wiltern Theater (along with the adjacent Pellissier Building) was rescued from demolition by the concerted efforts of local preservationists.

An exquisite example of Los Angeles deco, the Wiltern was restored by Wayne Ratkovich, principal of Ratkovich, Bowers & Perez, the same group who restored the Oviatt Building, a deco tower with retail and restaurant space.

Typical of many small deco theaters in Los Angeles, El Rey is a jazzy, white stucco structure. Its ticket booth floats above a sea of colorful terrazzo. El Rey is one of the few theaters that still has its original electric signage, ascribing to the following advice offered by E.C.A. Bullock: "Electric signs should be designed at the same time as the theater front thus avoiding . . . the obscuring . . . of a fine terra-cotta front or stone exterior by huge and ugly electric signs."[15] The Fox Wilshire, at 8440 Wilshire Blvd; the Roxie Theater, at 518 South Broadway; and the Fox-Warner Brothers Theater, at 478 West 6th Street in San Pedro, are other examples of this genre.

A B O V E
The color Pellissier green was created especially for the cladding of the twelve-story office complex and theater by Gladding McBean, terra-cotta manufacturers in Northern California.

A B O V E
In their sensuous curving movement, the stairs, balcony, and mezzanine reinforce the balustrade's wave motif.

L E F T
The tones of the oval mural crowning the lobby are evocative of the twilight colorations in paintings by Maxfield Parrish.

ABOVE
Stylistically foliated capitals adorn the mezzanine of the Wiltern Theater.

LEFT
The Wiltern's interior was restored to its former glamour by architects Brenda A. Levin and Maureen Sullivan in 1986. In place of the original orange color scheme, a pink, green, and burgundy scheme was chosen. The carpeting, some fixtures, and the theater seats are not original.

During the 1920s and 1930s, Avalon Bay on Santa Catalina Island was a favorite local resort, a refuge from the city where Big Band music could be heard in the evening and movies were screened nightly at the spacious Avalon Theater. The Casino was built by William Wrigley, Jr., the well-known chewing-gum magnate from Chicago. The Casino complex is cylindrical in shape. Two wings flank the entrance pavilion, providing access to the ballroom.

Thirty-two ceiling beams, a series of chandeliers, and a decorative grille form a vast, glittering sunburst over the parquet floors of the ballroom of the Catalina Island Casino, 1929, Webber and Spaulding.

21

Engaged columns are studded with elongated sconces in the Casino ballroom. Large headmolds are framed by silver-leaf swags and have octagonal figurative plaques.

22

LEFT
A cantilevered loggia, silhouetted by corbeled arches, surrounds the ballroom and imparts an exotic, Moorish feeling to the space. The ceiling features stenciling by theater artist John Gabriel Beckman, who was responsible for all the painted decoration in the Casino and Avalon Theater.

OPPOSITE
The entrance pavilion to the Avalon Theater is adorned with murals inspired by the views of underwater gardens and colorful fish and sea life seen on Santa Catalina Island's popular glass-bottom boat excursions.

ABOVE
The 1926-1927 Mayan Theater, located at
1040 South Hill Street, was designed by the
Morgan, Walls, Clements firm.

LEFT
Wrigley's development of Santa Catalina
Island was balanced by his support for the
preservation of its natural resources. To
encourage economic growth, he underwrote
the cost of establishing a local tileworks and
an island-based furniture factory and
developed a mining business. Storefronts
along an undulating beach walk in Avalon
are faced with the locally produced tiles.

ABOVE
The firm of Morgan, Walls, Clements produced a large number of Los Angeles buildings during the 1920s. Of these, the Mayan Theater is perhaps the most intricately designed.

RIGHT
Francisco Conejo sculpted these cast-concrete Mayan-style glyphs, warriors, and gods on the façade of the theater. The original impact of the façade was much more subdued, as the stuccowork was painted a subtle gray.

26

ABOVE
B. Marcus Priteca utilized sculptural elements on the façade of the 1929 Pantages Theater, at 6233 Hollywood Blvd., scene of the glittering Academy Awards ceremonies from 1949 to 1959.

LEFT
Floral motifs on the stucco façade of El Rey Theater are interpreted in neon, in a rare integration of lighting technology and the decorative arts at the time. The sign was clearly designed by the theater's architect, as opposed to the normal practice of adding neon signage to a theater as an afterthought.

ABOVE

An exotic temple of popular culture, Grauman's Chinese Theater, designed by Meyer and Holler, immediately became a mecca for movie fans. Norma Talmadge, Mary Pickford, and Douglas Fairbanks were the first to leave their handprints in the concrete of the forecourt at the theater's star-studded opening in 1927.

LEFT

Tiny copper dragons seem to run down the steep Oriental-style gables of the Chinese Theater, located at 6925 Hollywood Blvd.

TOP
Meyer and Holler merged flat, painted elements with the highly sculptural, fanciful forms on the façade of the Chinese Theater.

ABOVE
Metal tassels imitating silk hang from the theater's eaves.

ABOVE
The Chinese Theater has an expansive forecourt dominated by a red-roofed temple box office with wood-beam framing known as *chia liang*.

CHAPTER TWO

Residential Buildings

Los Angeles perhaps has the richest resources when it comes to the single-family, detached residence. Each house is a paradise unto itself. Man's "castles" are reflective of the individual's (or the architect's) tastes, desires, and eccentricities. Experimental housing has always had a place in Los Angeles, and the forms of the houses themselves, especially with regard to materials used and "open" plans, have been possible because of the pleasant climate.

Between 1917 and 1924, Frank Lloyd Wright and Irving Gill, two of the most influential American architects of the twentieth century, left their marks on domestic design in Los Angeles. Both started their careers in Louis Sullivan's Chicago office where they were exposed to Sullivan's innovative use of ornament and his practice of contrasting flat planes with geometric volumes. (Similar experiments were also taking place at the same time in Vienna.) Historian John A. Kouwenhoven has argued that the American and Viennese architectural movements were the result of exposure to vernacular design and industrial engineering. [16]

Between 1917 and 1924, Frank Lloyd Wright designed five textile-block houses in Los Angeles, each one strongly influenced by Mesoamerican temples and complexes. All five houses are stunningly decorative. Frank Lloyd Wright's son, Lloyd—an important architect in his own right with a bold yet lyrical style—was also influenced by Pre-Columbian architecture. The Sowden house of 1926, for example, originally contained

large steles in its courtyard.

The usual Los Angeles house, however, was not designed by an avant-garde architect but represented one or another type of revival style—American Colonial, Mediterranean, English Cottage, or French Provincial. Many movie stars, millionaires, and literati chose to live in extravagant revival-style houses but others were attracted to the modernistic style.

One of the most ambitious architect-designed projects was in a Los Angeles suburb, Torrance. In 1915, developer Jered Sidney Torrance hired landscape architects Olmsted and Olmsted to plan and landscape an industrial development to be named after the developer. Olmsted and Olmsted, in turn, prevailed upon Lloyd Wright (their employee at the time) to bring Irving Gill into the project. [17] The Torrance commission even-

tually enabled both Wright and his new associate, Gill, to move to Los Angeles, where Wright also supervised his father's projects, beginning with the Barnsdall residence known as Hollyhock house on Hollywood's Olive Hill.

Lloyd Wright's own emerging style can be seen in the 1922 Henry Bollman house at 1530 North Ogden Drive. In his use of knit block, Lloyd Wright demonstrated his ability to combine strong volumes with intricate massing and austere ornament. By 1923, when he designed the Taggart house, Lloyd Wright had mastered an organic approach to architecture. While supervising the construction of his father's textile-block houses, he gained a superior technical understanding of that material. By the late 1920s, Lloyd Wright was designing such masterpieces as the 1926–1928 Samuel-Navarro house (recently remodeled) and the Derby house, with its underground garage so integrated into the design that

LEFT
The Montecito Apartments, at 6650 Franklin Avenue, Hollywood, were built circa 1929 and have been the home to many aspiring movie stars.

OPPOSITE
Exquisite paneled walls, parquet floors, and Lalique light fixtures are seen in the penthouse atop Walker and Eisen's 1927–1928 Oviatt Building, at 617 South Olive Street in Downtown Los Angeles.

it appears to support the house above.

The garage was an integral part of the California house of the 1920s. A member of the Department of Commerce's Division of Building and Housing remarked in 1929 that "the automobile, besides permitting residences to spread out to suburban areas served by private cars . . . has affected the size, shape and features of the lot and of the house."[18]

So, too, did the ever-expanding bathroom. Inspired by their glamorous counterparts in movies, bathrooms in Los Angeles homes became larger and more sybaritic than ever before.

The Oviatt Building's penthouse residence has a marvelous bathroom, luxuriously clad with incised terra-cotta walls, with separate cubicles for bidets and toilets and a very large citron-tiled steam room, complete with a stainless-steel table. Each detail was especially fabricated for this room. James Oviatt, the original owner of the penthouse, visited the Paris "Art Deco" Exposition of 1925. Upon his return, he was determined to erect a new office tower with a retail shop at street level and a penthouse on the twelfth floor done in the modernistic style.[19]

The Oviatt Building was designed by the firm of Albert R. Walker and Percy A. Eisen, known for its Beaux-Arts buildings rich in Spanish Colonial and Gothic influences. Carl Jules Weyl, who was employed by the firm in the mid-1920s, also played an important part in the design.[20] During the late 1920s, Weyl designed several Art Deco-style buildings with his partner Henry L. Gogerty. While Walker and Eisen took care of the building's larger design, major details such as the entrance and elevator doors were designed by famed glass designer René Lalique. (In fact, the Oviatt Building was Lalique's largest commercial commission.)

32

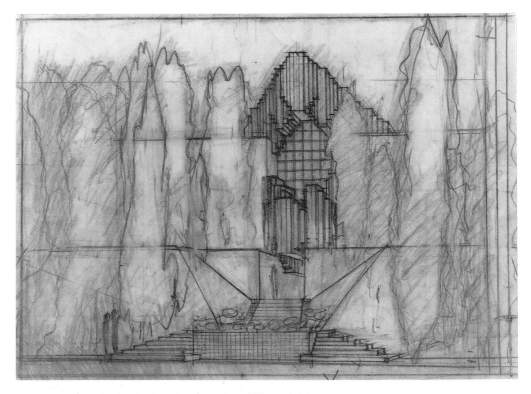

ABOVE
The Derby house, designed in 1926 by Lloyd Wright, has been exceptionally well restored by Pete Puvens, who worked with Lloyd Wright during the late 1960s. Textile-block screens on the south side shield the interior from the heat and glare of the sun.

LEFT
The multi-level Derby house is located at 2235 Chevy Chase Drive in Glendale. The sitting area on its entrance level is dominated by a fireplace with a fire screen featuring yucca motifs designed by the architect.

34

One wall of the Taggart house is lined with
built-in bookcases designed by Lloyd Wright.
The living-room furniture was designed by
the architect's father, Frank Lloyd Wright.

Stepped pyramid detailing, constructed of
wood and concrete, is seen on the exterior
of the Taggart residence.

The Taggart house, located in the Los Feliz
district of Los Angeles, was designed by
Lloyd Wright in 1922–1924. Its interior is
an example of Wright's total design concept,
with all fixtures and built-in furniture
designed specifically for the project.

ABOVE
Inspired by Japanese construction, steps lead down into a narrow open foyer adjacent to the main living area of the Taggart house.

RIGHT
On all sides, the house opens onto gardens and patios protected by overhangs at various levels.

ABOVE
The hallway ceiling of the Oviatt penthouse is painted midnight blue, with tiny gold stars illuminated by soffit lighting designed by Lalique. Photographs of movie stars on the walls are all inscribed to James Oviatt.

LEFT
A French marble mantel, the asymmetrical spider-web floor pattern on the parquet floor, and burled-walnut cornices make the main living room of the Oviatt penthouse a lavish example of the Art Deco style.

OPPOSITE
The large bathroom of the Oviatt penthouse has superbly executed walls of incised terra cotta, a large sunken bathtub, and a series of cubicles radiating from the central space that contain steam bath, bidet, and toilet. The entire room is illuminated by a magnificent Lalique-designed skylight.

ABOVE
During the 1920s, many Los Angeles apartment houses were designed in the deco style. The 1928 building at 570 Rossmore was inhabited by screen star Mae West for several years.

LEFT
The 1929 Los Feliz Manor Apartment Building, at 4643 Los Feliz Blvd., was designed by Jack Grunfors in the manner of the Wrights' textile-block structures.

OPPOSITE
Textured cast-concrete surfaces decorate the façade of Los Feliz Manor Apartments. The incised surfaces represent a stylized appropriation of the Wrights' aesthetic.

CHAPTER THREE

Public Buildings

Originally settled near a river, Los Angeles has a terrain composed of undulating hills surrounding a flat riverbed where its downtown is now located. The city's population explosion during the first few decades of the twentieth century prompted the construction of numerous schools, libraries, and police and fire stations. Plans for a new city hall designed by John C. Austin (who also worked on Griffith Observatory), John and Donald Parkinson, Albert C. Martin, and Austin Whittlesey, Associated Architects were approved in 1923.[21]

When completed in 1928, Los Angeles City Hall ushered in a new era of construction. It was the tallest building in the city, exceeding the 150-foot height limit a city ordinance imposed on structures. As a municipal building, however, the city hall building was exempt from this legislation. It has a theatrical profile, with a stepped pyramid at its pinnacle, derivative of the Mausoleum of Halicarnassus, one of the seven wonders of the ancient world. The rest of the building exhibits a mix of streamlined neoclassical and Spanish Colonial elements, with many references to local history. As architect and critic John Austin notes," . . . the architects [were] determined not to confine themselves to any particular design . . ."[22] The ornament on the bronze doors, he went on to explain, depict many "notable events in connection with the early history and settlement of Southern California, particularly, of Los Angeles."[23]

The Central Library is an influential building in

Los Angeles constructed during the 1920s. Its architect was Bertram Grosvenor Goodhue (architect Carleton Monroe Winslow supervised the building's construction). Lee Lawrie, a sculptor, worked closely with Goodhue to create the figurative ornaments surrounding the library's entrances. During this period, Lawrie and Goodhue also collaborated on the Nebraska State Capitol Building in Lincoln. In both cases, Lawrie's contributions enhance the spare buildings. "Nowhere is there an interruption that says, 'This is pedestal, that is image.'"[24]

In Los Angeles, Federal architecture is not as overpowering as it is in other areas of the United States, primarily because so many of the city's government buildings were built during the

1920s, the decade prior to the enactment of the Public Works Administration in 1932. Work produced under the auspices of the P.W.A. was required to be earthquake-proof. School layout and design were particularly affected by this requirement. Large schools, for example, were separated into a series of buildings connected to each other by means of metal slip joints or by arcades or passageways.[25]

Hollywood High School offers an example of this type of layout. The school's Household and Liberal Arts Building is separated from the Science Building and each is arranged in an L shape with wings (containing classrooms) attached by narrow passages. When built, Hollywood High School was considered an outstanding example of concrete construction and was illustrated in a two-page layout of Short and Stanley-Brown's *Public Buildings* book.

LEFT
Shaft detail, Los Angeles City Hall, 1928, John C. Austin, John and Donald Parkinson, Albert C. Martin, and Austin Whittlesey, located at the corner of Main and Temple Streets in Downtown Los Angeles.

OPPOSITE
The 1934–1935 Griffith Observatory dominates its hilltop site in Griffith Park. Designed by John C. Austin and Frederic M. Ashley, it is one of the most exciting structures in the Los Angeles area.

42   Strong, simple geometric forms characterize the exterior of the Griffith Observatory.

Griffith Observatory is one of the most successful public buildings in the city, in part due to its magnificent 3,000-acre site overlooking the Los Angeles basin. The land was given to the City of Los Angeles by Colonel Griffith J. Griffith, owner of Rancho Los Feliz.[26] With three domes, a central planetarium, and two flanking telescopes, the observatory is more opulent than many other similar structures from the 1930s, such as the Adler Planetarium in Chicago and the Planetarium in Dusseldorf, Germany. Inside the planetarium theater, in order to create the illusion of a celestial sky, a hemisphere rotates inside the roof's hemispherical ceiling. The outer roof need not necessarily be hemispherical; the roof of the Leipzig Planetarium, as an example, is pyramidal. But a rounded form does somehow more clearly express the building's purpose.[27]

TU TELESCOPE

ABOVE
A shell-like, curving stairway leads to the observation deck and telescopes.

LEFT
Transom grille and entrance grilles are decorated with various symbols related to astronomy.

LEFT
An arcade on the
southern side of the
building is lined with
small telescopes from
which to view the Los
Angeles basin.

The monolithic massing
of the Griffith
Observatory building
is lightened by
scalloping on the dome
walls and the zigzag
motif atop the
buttresses that form
the southern arcade.

ABOVE
Architects Donald B. Parkinson and J.M. Estep designed Santa Monica City Hall. The decorative tiles on the exterior are continued on the interior where a terrazzo mural reconstructs regional history.

ABOVE RIGHT
Santa Monica City Hall, 1685 Main Street, is a 1938 building that combines decorative art motifs and Streamlined forms.

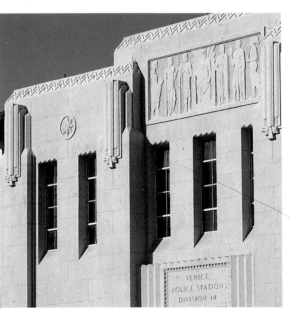

LEFT
The elegant Venice Police and Fire Station, on the corner of Venice Blvd. and Pisani Drive, boasts shell and wave motifs and an Egyptian-style bas relief above the police station entrance. The building dates from the early 1930s.

ABOVE
The façade of the 1937 Hollywood Post Office Branch, at 1615 Wilcox Avenue, is an excellent example of the Streamlined Moderne style as executed in Los Angeles.

ABOVE RIGHT
The post office was designed by Claude Beelman, one of the leading architects of deco-style buildings in Los Angeles, who collaborated on its design with the architecture-and-engineering firm Allison and Allison.

RIGHT
Beelman's distinctive decorative style is evident in the chunky, hieroglyphic floral band on the post office building.

A B O V E

Lee Lawrie's sculptures adorn the south entrance of the Los Angeles Central Library, located at the corner of South Flower and West 5th Streets. Designed by Bertram Goodhue and built between 1922–1926, the building influenced many others, including City Hall. Today it has fallen into disrepair, having suffered damage from fires and other catastrophes, and its future is threatened as surrounding high-rise development makes its value as real estate soar.

L E F T

The 1930 Los Angeles branch of the Federal Reserve Bank of San Francisco, located on the northwest corner of South Olive Street and West Olympic Blvd., was designed by John and Donald B. Parkinson. While a student at MIT, Parkinson was exposed to modernist theories. Upon his return to Los Angeles to practice architecture with his father's office, he guided the firm toward the use of the modernist aesthetic.

A B O V E

Hollywood High School, at 1521 North Highland Avenue, was built in 1935 with funds provided by the Public Works Administration. Two sculptural reliefs by Bartolo Mako mark its two entrances. The school was built by Marsh, Smith and Powell, a firm responsible for a number of Los Angeles area schools constructed during the 1930s.

47

CHAPTER FOUR

Ecclesiastical Buildings

L os Angeles, the "City of Angels," has been a haven for religious groups ever since the early 1930s. Transcendentalists and individuals who created their own religions were drawn to this paradisiacal place, building their own versions of the house of God. Nationally famous evangelist Aimee Semple McPherson, for example, constructed the 1925 Angelus Temple.[28]

Special attention was paid to funerary facilities, with their own kind of religious associations. Forest Lawn in Glendale became so extensive that it was rebuilt and expanded to connect with the Memorial Terrace in 1932. Hollywood Memorial Park Cemetery, at 6000 Santa Monica Blvd., surrounded by film studios, is hidden away from commercial activity by high walls. The cemetery's Egyptian-style temples and mausoleums, reflecting pool, and scattered palm trees impart a timeless quality to the setting.

Given Los Angeles's booming growth, urban land was soon deemed too expensive to be devoted to cemeteries and mausoleums. The suburb of Glendale, the site of Forest Lawn, was sufficiently distant from the downtown area so that land could be purchased inexpensively. Boyle Heights, to the east of Downtown Los Angeles, also offered less expensive real estate—one reason why the New Calvary Cemetery and Ross Montgomery's Mausoleum of the Golden West were located there.

Churches and synagogues, on the other hand,

were often located on prime commercial real estate. There is one section of Wilshire Blvd., consisting primarily of religious structures, that is a sort of Miracle Mile unto itself. Temple B'nai B'rith, now the Wilshire Boulevard Temple, is one of the most spectacular ecclesiastical buildings on this stretch.

Within the Jewish faith, a synagogue is defined as a minyan, or quorum, of ten males over the age of thirteen, rather than a specific building. Thus, Jews fleeing to the United States to seek religious freedom were not constricted by traditional building types when it came to designs for their synagogues.[29] Orientalism was one of the most popular styles employed in the design of American synagogues, first emerging in synagogue design in Philadelphia, then taking root in New York City. Henry Fernbach designed the first axial-domed synagogue in the United States, the late-

1860s temple for the Shaaray Tefila congregation in New York City.[30]

By the time Temple B'nai B'rith (now Wilshire Boulevard Temple) was built in Los Angeles, the axial dome had become an accepted form. B'nai B'rith's dome, originally clad in bright terra-cotta tiles, is 100 feet in diameter and rises to a height of 135 feet. Designed by A.M. Edelman with the architecture and engineering firm of Allison and Allison to withstand the force of earthquakes, B'nai B'rith was constructed out of concrete using the cement-gun process.[31]

Not all synagogues were revivalist in style, however. Two synagogues and several Roman Catholic churches in the Los Angeles area built during the early decades of the twentieth century were realized in a modernistic style. The B'nai David Synagogue in Baldwin Hills is a textbook example of how geometric form and pattern can be successfully applied to ecclesiastical structures. Our Lady of Lourdes, a Roman Catholic

LEFT
An exquisite balance between sculpture and massing is apparent on the facade of Ross Montgomery's 1927 Mausoleum of the Golden West, at 4201 East Whittier Blvd. in the Boyle Heights area.

OPPOSITE
Hugo Ballin's murals adorn the interior of A.M. Edelman's 1929 Wilshire Boulevard Temple, at 3663 Wilshire Blvd.

church at 3773 East Third Street in Boyle Heights, is a very good, if somewhat subdued, example of the regional deco style.

Concrete was the perfect medium for these two religious buildings; it was wonderfully sculptable (allowing for geometric massing), inexpensive, and capable of withstanding earthquakes when reinforced. Concrete appealed to architects working in the deco style because its cast edges resembled those found in more expensive cut or carved stone. In his article, "Architectural Concrete—Forms, Molds and Surfaces," William C. Wagner, an architect with the firm of Morgan, Walls, Clements, describes the technical advantages of working with concrete to form ornament.[32] Waste molds—plaster casts discarded after use—were employed to create the elaborately detailed Spanish Colonial or Churrigueresque decoration.

When a design was simple and geometric with little undercutting, wooden molds could be used over and over again, reducing the cost of decoration. To some extent, this may explain why the Spanish Colonial revival style was finally superseded by deco styles during the late 1920s.

51

OPPOSITE
The Wilshire Boulevard Temple (formerly Temple B'nai B'rith) exudes a massive presence. Its detailing is a mixture of Renaissance influences and regional deco motifs, such as the geometric wave at the crown of the dome.

ABOVE
The auditorium of the Wilshire Boulevard Temple has corbeled beams and a frescoed ceiling. Open terra-cotta grilles conceal ventilation shafts.

LEFT
An Oriental opulence pervades the Wilshire Boulevard Temple's sanctuary, enhanced by Byzantine columns and a coffered ceiling.

ABOVE
The Church of the Blessed Sacrament, at 6657 Sunset Blvd. in Hollywood, was designed in the mid-1920s by T. Franklin Power and the Beezer Brothers of Seattle.

LEFT
The striking decorative program on the church's tower blends deco- and Mission revival-style elements.

OPPOSITE
Chapels flank steps leading to the entrance to the Mausoleum of the Golden West.

RIGHT
Vaults are placed
under bilateral arcades
on the northern side of
the Mausoleum of the
Golden West building.

ABOVE
The Mausoleum of the Golden West is one of the best examples of L.A. deco style. The stained-glass windows in the family vaults were fabricated by Judson Studios.

ABOVE RIGHT
The pyramidal ceiling of the Ross Montgomery-designed Mausoleum of the Golden West at the New Calvary Cemetery hovers above an entrance leading to a chapel and to wings containing vaults.

LEFT
Palm leaf grilles over the windows shield the interior from the light from the southern exposure. The parapet grilles are purely ornamental.

ABOVE
Traditional Christian iconography has been
rendered in a stylized manner reflective of
the architecture of the Mausoleum of the
Golden West.

LEFT
Acanthus leaves, swirling foliage, and exotic
birds, all molded from cast concrete, decorate
the parapet of the mausoleum.

OPPOSITE
B'nai David Synagogue, at Swall Drive and
Pico Blvd., built circa 1929, is an excellent
example of the deco concrete style as applied
to ecclesiastical architecture.

CHAPTER FIVE

Commercial Buildings

Until the creation of Miracle Mile, Downtown Los Angeles was the center of the city's commercial and social activity. But as the downtown area was increasingly congested by traffic and trolley cars, the area became less attractive to shoppers.

In 1921, real estate developer A.W. Ross was one of the first to take note of this shift and responded by creating a shopping district on Wilshire Blvd., on what were then open bean fields between La Brea and Fairfax Avenues. Within a few years, shoppers from Beverly Hills, Hollywood, West Adams Heights, and Hancock Park—all expensive residential areas—were drawn to this shopping area, soon to be known as Miracle Mile.[33] To attract shoppers who came by car, all the shops and department stores were designed with rear parking lots, as curbside parking on Wilshire Blvd. was prohibited. Traffic signals were synchronized and streets were widened with landscaped islands to keep traffic moving and the street attractive and to make the stores as accessible by automobile as possible.

Other developers followed Ross's example and small shopping districts were created in nearby Baldwin Hills, in Los Feliz, and in Beverly Hills. At the same time, the downtown area continued to grow as many skyscrapers—those unique icons of American architecture—were built. By the late 1920s, the Broadway-Spring Arcade Building, the Bank of America, and the Title Insurance and Trust Building had been built in the financial dis-

trict along Spring Street.

In 1929 construction began on the Pacific Coast Stock Exchange, designed by Samuel E. Lunden and the Parkinson and Parkinson firm. A sculptural program was executed by Salvatore Cartaino Scarpitta. Soon after finishing this building, Parkinson and Parkinson designed the Banks-Huntly Building across the street.

During this boom period, the Los Angeles Times Building was also under construction. James Ferguson, in a 1935 review for *Architect and Engineer*, claimed that the design of the Times Building resembled that of a group of buildings in the Civic Center—the State Building, City Hall, and the Federal Building.[34] Actually, the Times Building is a much more pleasing building than any of those with which he compares it. The Fed-

eral Building, by Gilbert Stanley Underwood, for instance, does not represent the architect's best work: Underwood was freer in his role as the consulting architect for the Union Pacific Railroad in the 1920s. Except for its decorative metalwork, the Federal Building poorly demonstrates Underwood's talent.

During the 1920s, skyscrapers were rising all over Downtown Los Angeles. Architect Claude Beelman was in such demand he had two buildings facing each other; Ninth and Broadway at 849 South Broadway and Eastern Columbia, a masterpiece of Los Angeles skyscraper style. So many buildings were going up at this time that Bruce Bliven, writing for *The New Republic* in 1927, recorded that

figures can't give any real sense of this choking jungle growth of people . . . my friend, the advertising man, with whom I talked recently on the thirteenth-floor of a brand-new skyscraper, which had been built, if not overnight, at least over the weekend . . . showed me the layout of a souvenir booklet he was preparing . . .

LEFT AND OPPOSITE
Gordon B. Kaufman was the architect of the 1935 Los Angeles Times Building, at 210 West First Street in Downtown Los Angeles. Both the Art Deco and Streamlined styles were embraced in this imposing structure, designed to accommodate both editorial offices and printing production facilities.

ABOVE
Clocks were a popular and utilitarian tower ornament applied to Los Angeles skyscrapers. The clock atop the Los Angeles Times Building faces in the direction of nearby Federal buildings. Decorative concrete grilles are also typical regional building features, which here technically and aesthetically lighten the tower's overall mass.

he had before him two contrasting photographs of the city's skyline. They were called 'The Old' and 'The New'; and they looked as much alike, say, as Vienna and Chicago. The new one was taken, I saw in 1926, but what about the other, the prehistoric perspective? 'It is,' said my friend, 'an ancient view I dug up out of a desk drawer'. It shows the skyline in 1922.[35]

The elegant Bullock's Wilshire department store became synonymous with luxury and service. It is John and Donald B. Parkinson's masterpiece, entirely clad in beige terra cotta manufactured by Gladding, McBean & Company of Lincoln, California.[36] The motor entrance was originally designed to have a brightly colored faience mural surrounding the decorative iron transom and door grilles. Stepped back at the corners, with an asymmetrically located tower, the store's façade is entirely decorated with geometric motifs.

A review of Bullock's in *Architect and Engineer* discussed the structure in terms of the zoning laws:

Owing to the strategic location on Wilshire Boulevard, it was found desirable to create a tower on the building for the advertising value such a lofty landmark would possess. The Los Angeles Building Ordinance permits but a 150 foot building height limit. However, in addition to this height, the law permits six feet of roof construction, 35 feet of penthouse construction and 50 feet of sign construction, making a total possible legal height of 241 feet. The penthouse structure can be used only for tanks and machinery, while the sign structure must be for advertising purposes only. As the law further restricts the sign structure to the use of sheet metal and light steel members, this feature, to a great extent, determined the design of the entire building. It was thought undesirable to paint the upper 50 feet of the tower in imitation of terra-cotta masonry used in the lower stories of the building and as it was most desirable to tie the crowning feature of the tower into the remainder of the building, the metal finish of the so-called sign structure was carried through all of the spandrels, thereby determining to a great extent the actual forms used in the design as well as the color. The green of oxidized copper and the buff colored terra-cotta that were selected, form a combination of color that seems to fit in very happily with the California atmosphere.[37]

Many of the details of the Bullock's Wilshire are the result of the Parkinson firm's collaboration with other architects and designers. Jock Peters, known for several deco-style houses in the San Fernando Valley, worked on the department store's interior with the interior design firm of Feil and Paradice.

The modern art editor of *Architect and Engineer,* raving about the building, wrote:

To my mind it is one of the most consistently modern creations in large retail stores in this country. There has been a handling of materials that reflects a fine sense of their natural beauty . . . . Throughout, the beautiful craftsmanship is evident, reflecting in the assembly of the materials an appreciation of modern form and principal of design. Retail merchandising offers a fruitful field for originality on the part of the modernist. The success of this particular store from a merchandising standpoint, aside from architecture, is clearly shown in the crowds surging around the building at night and through it during the day and that all California is talking about it.[38]

61

ABOVE
Sculpted from California pink granite, this eagle rests permanently on the Times Building.

LEFT
Monumental in scope, the Los Angeles Times Building required 150,000 sacks of cement and 35,000 tons of rock and sand during construction.

ABOVE LEFT
The 1929 Wilshire Professional Building, at 3875 Wilshire Blvd., was designed by Arthur E. Harvey. New storefronts have covered the original wrought-iron grilles on its first floor.

ABOVE
Cast-concrete and metal details embellish the façade of the Wilshire Professional Building.

LEFT
Curved piers are an innovative aspect of the building's design.

A B O V E
Claude Beelman's Garfield Building, at 408
West 8th Street in Downtown Los Angeles,
dates from 1930. Its lobby is richly clad in
red and black marble, with gold-leafed
plaster cornices and elevator floor
indicators flanked by stylized nudes.

L E F T
Over the entrance to Beelman's Garfield
Building is a canopy ceiling decorated with
a radiating sun design.

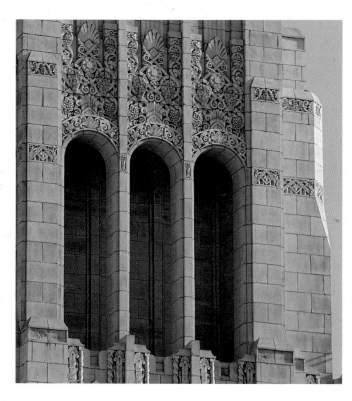

ABOVE
Spandrels on the Garfield Building add further to the established solar motif.

LEFT
The tower of the Garfield Building is clad in foliated terra cotta. Stylized palm fronds and grape clusters form the primary motifs of this frothy structure.

Scenes of the region's
history and palm trees
decorate the entrance
and first two floors of
the Los Angeles First
National Bank
Building, a 1927
Meyer and Holler
design, located at
6777 Hollywood Blvd.

BELOW
Forceful modeling and
sculpture make the
Pacific Coast Stock
Exchange, 1929–
1930, Samuel Lunden
and the Parkinson firm,
stand out among
neighboring structures.
It is located at 618
South Spring Street.

65

ABOVE
One of the few tall buildings on Highland
Avenue, the Los Angeles First National Bank
Building (now Security Pacific National Bank)
is visible from afar. The octagonal tower with
projecting gargoyles makes this building a
particularly flamboyant presence.

LEFT
Oriental lions project just above the seventh-
story setback of the Los Angeles First National
Bank Building in Hollywood.

RIGHT
John and Donald Parkinson's 1931 Title and Guarantee Building, at the northwest corner of South Hill and West 5th Streets, has a tower partially composed of a terra-cotta screen.

BELOW
Arthur Harvey's Selig Retail Store, circa 1928, at Western Avenue and West 3rd Street, is a glamourous study in black and gold terra cotta.

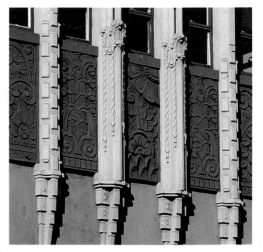

ABOVE TOP
Single-story stucco structures with a faint touch of Art Deco abound in Los Angeles. This circa 1930 building is located on the corner of Willoughby and La Brea Avenues.

ABOVE
With its curvilinear pilasters and volutes, the Owl Drug Store Building, circa 1930, at the southwest corner of Wilshire and Robertson Blvds., may be the work of local architect Arthur Harvey.

LEFT
Bullock's Wilshire (now
I. Magnin), designed
by Parkinson and
Parkinson, Jock Peters,
and Feil and Paradice
in 1929, is located at
3050 Wilshire Blvd.,
in the Mid-Wilshire
area of Los Angeles.
The tower—the store's
classic signature and a
form of advertising—is
integral to the overall
design of the building.

RIGHT
Cantilevers protect the
display windows of
the Bullock's Wilshire
store from the sun's
fading rays. The curling
wave and fan motifs
make these more than
utilitarian forms.

ABOVE
The ceiling of the porte-cochère at the rear of
the Bullock's store was painted by Herman
Sachs; it depicts Los Angeles's best-known
industries—aviation, shipping, and railroads—
as well as water and plant motifs.

RIGHT
Fabulous cast-iron gates lead to the porte-
cochère and the main entrance at the rear of
Bullock's Wilshire.

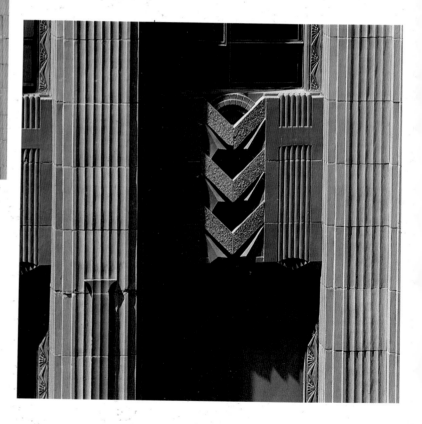

ABOVE
Unlike the carefully preserved Bullock's Wilshire, the Eastern Columbia Building is in need of serious restoration work.

RIGHT
Beelman favored floral ornamentation; this landmark building is one of the few he designed that is strictly geometric.

OPPOSITE
Claude Beelman also designed Ninth and Broadway, the building directly across the street from the Eastern Columbia Building; both were built in 1929.

74

ABOVE
The cast-concrete sheathing on the tower of Ninth and Broadway is intended to replicate the look of the cast terra cotta on the lower floors of the building.

LEFT
Use of a geometric Gothic pendant contrasts with the ornate terra-cotta foliation of Ninth and Broadway, entirely clad in this material except for its tower.

LEFT
A one-story commercial building with tower to attract a motorist's attention, located at the southeast corner of Beverly Blvd. and Poinsettia, was designed in 1930 by architect J.R. Horns.

BELOW
The Security First National Bank of Los Angeles, 1929, was designed by the firm Morgan, Walls, Clements. Cast-aluminum grilles complement black terra-cotta cladding on this building located at 5209 Wilshire Blvd., Beverly Hills.

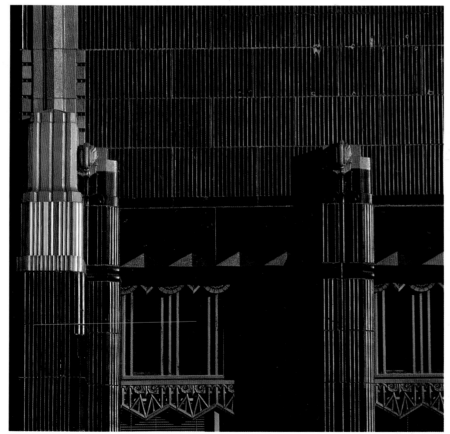

75

ABOVE **T**OP
The Elks Building (now the Park Plaza Hotel), at 607 South Park View Street, is one of Claude Beelman's earliest experiments in deco imagery in Los Angeles. Working with William Curlett, the architect completed the building in 1924.

ABOVE
The massing of the Elks Building is vaguely Secessionist in style.

CHAPTER SIX

Metal Details

hough concrete was the favored material for deco-style buildings in the Los Angeles area, many interesting details are found on metal doors, grilles, and lighting fixtures, a switch from the lacy wrought-iron details frequently used on the Spanish Colonial revival-style buildings in the city. Many deco buildings had entrances that gained great formality by the use of decorative grilles, transoms or doors.

Copper, anodized to a bright sea-green, is often seen on roofs. The metal could be unusually shaped due to its malleability. Brass, which retains its warm golden color, was often cast to form elevator doors. Aluminum, first applied to buildings during the 1920s, was used primarily for structural details and sometimes replaced more expensive silver or gold as a leafing material. The extrusion process encouraged the use of bronze for window surrounds and door jambs and moldings.

An article in *Architect and Engineer* suggested that because of climatic factors, open grillwork was particularly suited for use in buildings in Southern California: "Iron, and any other architectural metal, is the one material that will permit the greatest reduction of cross section . . . and permits the largest area of free or open space in design."[39]

Metal fences and grilles, seen often on period buildings in Los Angeles, provided a sense of privacy while also allowing for the penetration of light and air.

76

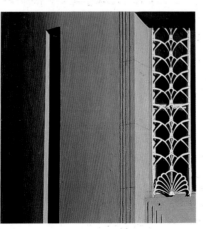

LEFT
The ornament on the 1929–1931 Parkinson and Parkinson-designed Banks–Huntly building, at 632 South Spring Street, is Streamlined and simplified.

BELOW LEFT
A wrought-iron seashell motif decorates a window grille on a circa 1933 building at the southeast corner of Yucca and Vine Streets in Hollywood.

OPPOSITE
A stylized aluminum cornice with glass portions designed by the renowned René Lalique illuminates the foyer of the Oviatt Building, located at 617 South Olive Street in Downtown Los Angeles.

ABOVE
Detail, brass lintel above the elevator door in the lobby of the Banks–Huntly Building.

RIGHT
Elements of the essential California landscape—sea, hills, and sun—are etched on the elevator doors in the lobby of the Garfield Building.

OPPOSITE
The Oviatt Building's lobby is open to the street, protected by decorative wrought-iron and brass grilles.

OPPOSITE
A circa 1929 building, at 1545 Wilcox Avenue in Hollywood, combines metal transoms with terra-cotta cladding.

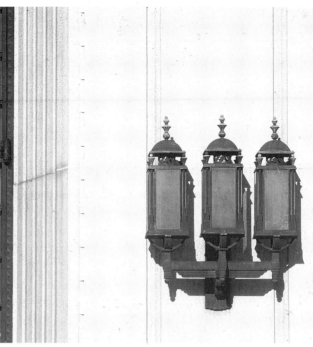

ABOVE
Bronze spandrels and window frames appear on the Eastern Columbia Building.

TOP RIGHT
Bronze lamp fixtures flank the entrance to the Federal Reserve Building, 1930, Parkinson and Parkinson, located at the corner of Olive Street and Olympic Blvd.

RIGHT
The Hollywood Post Office offers cast-aluminum spandrels and a medallion depicting Mercury.

CHAPTER SEVEN

Waves, Seashells, Flowers, and Towers

The Los Angeles incarnation of Art Deco is an exuberant style incorporating indigenous elements, curling waves, rustling palm trees, Hollywood glamour, and automobile motifs. In the same manner as the Spanish Colonial and Mission revival styles, deco details reveal a clear expression of place.

Even though Miami has a similar climate, the differences between deco buildings in Miami and those in Los Angeles are clearly visible. The Hollywood-influenced taste for glitter created a desire for lush façades of gold, black, and other dramatic colors. Blue and green were also frequently used, especially in the tones typical of the waters of Santa Monica Bay. Structurally sound, colorful, and fire-resistant, terra cotta—also resistant to fading—was one of the signature materials applied to Los Angeles deco buildings.

Streamlined design, with its implied vibrant sense of movement and energy, had a great impact on the architecture of Los Angeles, a city that evolved, in large part, in response to the automobile. W. Francklyn Paris, in a review of the Paris Exposition, stated that

"Speed is not only expressed in movement, it begets a state of mind, and since curves are eloquent of repose and languor they no longer find a place in modern architecture or in the composition of surrounding objects which serve as a setting for our daily life."[40]

Along Miracle Mile, numerous businesses se-

lected the Art Deco as the new image with which to attract customers. The style rapidly spread to the suburbs as the predominant commercial style.

Other typical Los Angeles imagery, such as foliation, scenes of Paradise, nudes, and fruit and grape clusters, have little similarity to those found in French Art Deco buildings. They reflect both the American experience and the unique flavor of Southern California. Several motifs, such as the bilaterally symmetrical fountain, are derivative of French design, but even so, they offer a California twist, with the addition of birds, a familiar paradisiacal element.

The sea and seashore also inspired numerous local deco motifs—seashells, crabs and fish, mermaids, and mythological figures associated with

LEFT
The local building code mandated the insertion of tie rods into pre-existing concrete structures to increase seismic resistance. Unfortunately these regulations sometimes marred attractive tile ornament, as at the circa 1929 building on the corner of Beverly Blvd. and Serrano Street.

OPPOSITE
A terra-cotta Neptune rules the entrance of the circa 1929 building at the northwest corner of 7th Street and Broadway.

the ocean, such as Neptune. The fabulous Sunset Tower Apartment Building and the Casino on Catalina Island offer examples of regional aquatic designs. Prominent motifs adapted from Egyptian, Chinese, or Spanish Mission styles also exerted their influence, in part due to their use in movies and their role in the cultures of newly settled ethnic groups in the area. When Los Angeles began building an aqueduct in the early twentieth century (at the time the largest project of its kind in the world), the activity provided a new awareness of ancient culture and popularized the use of Egyptian, Assyrian, and Babylonian motifs. Not only was Los Angeles the center of celluloid, it was also a physical paradise as well, where it was possible to grow oranges and house plants as large as trees, own a home, and seemingly live a carefree life forever.

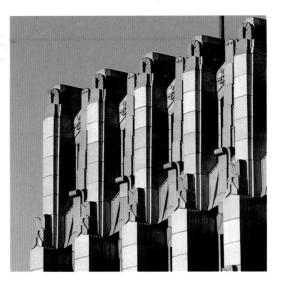

ABOVE
Curling geometric waves are depicted on the polychrome terra-cotta façade belonging to the 1928 J.J. Newberry store, located at 6600 Hollywood Blvd.

ABOVE **R**IGHT
The circa 1928 tower at 619 South Hill Street is clad in turquoise terra cotta.

RIGHT
Foliated and bracketed piers and spandrels counteract Cubistic elements atop the 619 South Hill Street Building.

ABOVE
Even a small tower attracts visibility. This 1930s automobile showroom building is located at 9030 Wilshire Blvd.

LEFT
The 1930s tower at 356 South Western Avenue is highly visible from blocks away.

ABOVE

The Max Factor Building, at 1666–68
Highland Avenue, remodeled by S. Charles
Lee in 1931, is a fitting symbol that seems
to capture the glamour of both the cosmetics
and film industries.

LEFT

Stucco seashells decorate the entrance of a
circa 1932 building at 616 La Brea Avenue.

ABOVE
John Beckman's murals for the Avalon
Theater's arcade fancifully depict a mermaid
swimming in a colorful underwater region.

RIGHT
Originally the S.H. Kress store, this 1935
building designed by Edward F. Sibbert has a
lacy floral, cast-concrete façade that conceals,
appropriately enough, the Frederick's of
Hollywood lingerie emporium.

ABOVE
Gogerty and Weyl's 1928 Yucca-Vine
Tower Building, on the northwest corner
of the same streets, integrates floral
and geometric ornament in a novel way.

LEFT
The circa 1928 300 Wilshire Boulevard
Building offers fleur-de-lis panels that
alternate with cast-concrete Art Deco-
style panels.

NOTES
▼

INTRODUCTION

1. Bevis Hillier, *Art Deco* (London: Studio Vista, 1968).
2. One indication of the battle waged between modernism and traditionalism can be found in a series of articles written by some of America's leading architects of the 1930s, presented in the magazine *Pencil Points* in 1932. See Albert H. Kahn, "An Approach to Design," *Pencil Points* 8 (May 1932), 299–301; Myron Hunt, "A Brief Comment from California," *Pencil Points* 8 (May 1932), 301–302; Alfred Fellheimer, "Contemporary Design in Architecture," *Pencil Points* 13 (June 1932), 383–389. Popular modernity was promoted by Paul T. Frankl in his book, *Form and Reform* (New York: Harper and Bros., 1930); and by Sheldon Cheney in his volume, *The New World Architecture* (London, New York, and Toronto: Longmans, Green and Co., 1930).
3. David Gebhard and Harriette von Breton, *Kem Weber: The Moderne in Southern California, 1920–1941* (Santa Barbara: University Art Museum, 1969).
4. David Gebhard, *Schindler* (Salt Lake City: Peregrine Smith, Inc., 1980), 73–75.
5. Frank Lloyd Wright, "In the Cause of Architecture VII, The Meaning of Materials—Concrete," *Architectural Record* 64 (October 1928), 334–342.
6. Anson B. Cutts, Jr., "The Hillside House of Ramon Navarro, A Unique setting created by Lloyd Wright," *California Arts and Architecture* 44 (July 1933), 11–13, 31. For a general discussion of Lloyd Wright, see David Gebhard and Harriette von Breton, *Lloyd Wright Architect* (Santa Barbara: University Art Museum, 1971).
7. David Gebhard and Harriette von Breton, *Los Angeles in the Thirties: 1931–1941* (Los Angeles: Hennessey and Ingalls, 1989), 75–92.

CHAPTER 1

1. David Lavender, *California: Land of New Beginnings* (New York: Harper & Row, 1972), 236.
2. Donald Albrecht, *Designing Dreams: Modern Architecture in the Movies* (New York: Harper & Row, 1986), 40.
3. Ibid, 43.
4. Ibid, 39.
5. C.H. Crane, " Observations on Motion Picture Theaters," *Architectural Record* (June, 1925), 381.

6. Robert Alleman, *The Movie Lover's Guide to Hollywood* (New York: Harper & Row, 1985), 177.
7. G. Albert Lansburgh, "The El Capitan Theater and Department Store Building, Hollywood," *Architect and Engineer* (February 1927), 37.
8. E.C.A. Bullock, "Theater Entrances and Lobbies," *Architectural Record* (June, 1925), 370.
9. Patricia Anne Moore, *The Casino, Avalon, California* (Avalon: Catalina Island Museum Society, Inc., 1979), 37.
10. Sumner A. Spaulding, "The Pleasure Isle of Catalina, Developing Avalon as a California Seashore Resort," *California Arts and Architecture* (November 1929), 74.
11. Kevin Starr, *Material Dreams: Southern California Through The 1920s* (New York: Oxford University Press, 1990), 98.
12. E.C.A. Bullock, "Theater Entrances," 370.
13. "The Planning of the Motion Picture Theater," *Architectural Forum* (June 1925), 385.
14. D.W. Hlava, *The Wiltern* (Los Angeles: Los Angeles Conservancy, 1986), unpaginated.
15. E.C.A. Bullock, "Theater entrances," 370.

CHAPTER 2

16. John A. Kouwenhoven, *Half a Truth is Better than None* (Chicago: University of Chicago Press, 1982), 98–100.
17. David Gebhard and Robert Winter, *Architecture in Los Angeles: A Compleat Guide* (Salt Lake City: Peregrine Smith, 1985), 90.
18. J.S. Taylor, "New Trends in Home Design," *Architect and Engineer* (August 1929), 87.
19. R. Hubert, "There's Lots of Room at the Top of This Building," *Los Angeles Times* (June 5, 1988), Section 8, 1,9.
20. Donald J. Schippers, "Walker & Eisen: Twenty Years of Los Angeles Architecture, 1920–1940," *The Historical Society of Southern California Quarterly* (June 1966), 381.

CHAPTER 3

21. John C. Austin, "The Los Angeles City Hall," *Architectural Forum* (September 1928), 25.
22. Ibid, 25.
23. Ibid, 26.
24. H.B. Alexander, "The Sculpture of Lee Lawrie,"

Architectural Forum (May 1931), 596.
25. C.W. Short and R. Stanley-Brown, *Public Buildings: A Survey of Architecture of Projects Constructed by Federal and Other Government Bodies Between the Years 1933 and 1939* (Washington, D.C.: U.S. Government Printing Office), XII.
26. Starr, *Material Dreams*, 111.
27. A.T. North, "The Adler Planetarium, Chicago," *Architectural Forum* (February 1931), 144.

CHAPTER 4

28. Gebhard and Winter, *Architecture in Los Angeles*, 191.
29. R. Wischnitzer, *Synagogue Architecture in the United States: History and Interpretation* (Philadelphia: The Jewish Publication Society of America, 1955), 3.
30. Ibid, 84.
31. "The New B'nai B'rith Temple, Los Angeles," *Architect and Engineer* (July 1929), 95.
32. W.C. Wagner, "Architectural Concrete Forms, Molds and Surfaces," *Architect and Engineer* (June 1931), 59.

CHAPTER 5

33. Starr, *Material Dreams*, 81–82.
34. J.K. Ferguson, "New Plant," *Architect and Engineer* (March 1935), 47.
35. Bruce Bliven, "Los Angeles: The City that is Bacchanalian—In A Nice Way," *The New Republic* (July 13, 1927).
36. G.F. Kurutz, "Murals in Tile—The Decorative Tile of Gladding, McBean & Co.," *California State Library Foundation Bulletin* (January 1989).
37. "Bullock's Wilshire Boulevard Store—Los Angeles," *Architect and Engineer* (December 1929), 45.
38. Ibid, 48–49.

CHAPTER 6

39. W. I. Garren, "Civilization: Metal and Architects," *Architect and Engineer* (February 1930), 43.

CHAPTER 7

40. W. Francklyn Paris, "The International Exposition of Modern Industrial and Decorative Art in Paris," *Architectural Record* (October 1925), 370. .

BIBLIOGRAPHY
▼

Albrecht, Donald. *Designing Dreams: Modern Architecture in the Movies.* New York: Harper & Row, 1986.

Alleman, Robert. *The Movie Lover's Guide to Hollywood.* New York: Harper & Row, 1985.

Arwas, Victor. *Art Deco.* London: Academy Editions, 1976.

Austin, Mary. *Land of Little Rain.* Boston: Little, Brown and Company, 1904.

Banham, Reyner. *Design By Choice.* New York: Rizzoli International Publications, 1981.

———. *Los Angeles: The Architecture of Four Ecologies.* New York: Viking Penguin, 1973.

———. *Scenes in America Deserta.* Salt Lake City: Peregrine Smith, 1982.

———. *Theory and Design in the First Machine Age.* New York: The Architectural Press, 1960.

Battersby, Martin. *The Decorative Thirties.* London: Studio Vista, 1971.

Beach, John. "Lloyd Wright's Sowden House, Bizarre Shapes from Custom-Cast Concrete Blocks." *Fine Homebuilding* (April–May 1983): 66–73.

Behrens, Peter. *Sein Werk von 1909 bis sur gegenwart Zusammengestell und gesschreiben von Paul Joseph Crenas.* Essen: G.D. Baedeker, 1928.

Bennett, T.P. *Architectural Design in Concrete.* London: E. Benn, Ltd., 1927.

Bingham, E. "Grauman Theater a Work of Art." *Architect and Engineer* (June 1923): 76–104.

Blake, Peter. *The Master Builders: Le Corbusier, Mies van der Rohe, Frank Lloyd Wright.* New York: W. W. Norton, 1976.

Boorstin, Daniel J. *The Image: A Guide to Pseudo-Events in America.* New York: Atheneum, 1987.

Bossom, Alfred C. "America's National Architecture." *American Architect* (July 24, 1925): 77–83.

Bragdon, Claude. *Architecture and Democracy.* New York: Alfred A. Knopf, 1918.

Bush, Donald J. *The Streamlined Decade.* New York: George Braziller, 1975.

Carlson, Marvin. *Palaces of Performance: The Semiotics of Theater Architecture.* Ithaca, NY: Cornell University Press, 1989.

Cheney, Sheldon. *The New World Architecture.* New York: Langmans, Green, 1930.

Fitch, James Marston. *American Building: The Historical Forces That Shaped It.* New York: Schocken Books, 1973.

Frampton, Kenneth. *Modern Architecture: A Critical History.* New York: Oxford University Press, 1980.

Frankl, Paul T. *Form and Re-Form.* New York: Harper & Brothers, 1930.

Garren, William I. "Modernism or The Architect's Speak-easy." *Architect and Engineer* (June 1929): 53–54.

Gebhard, David and Robert Winter. *Architecture in Los Angeles: A Compleat Guide.* Salt Lake City: Peregrine Smith, 1985.

Gebhard, David and Harriette von Breton. *L.A. in the Thirties.* Salt Lake City: Peregrine Smith, 1975.

Gill, Brendan. *Many Masks: A Life of Frank Lloyd Wright.* New York: G. P. Putnam's Sons, 1987.

Hailey, Genevieve. "California Shows Progress in the Decorative Arts." *Architect and Engineer* (May 1929): 91–93.

Hamlin, Talbot F. "California Ways & Wherefores." *Pencil Points* 22 (May 1914): 338–344.

Hitchcock, Henry-Russell. *In the Nature of Materials: The Buildings of Frank Lloyd Wright, 1887–1941.* New York: Hawthorn Books, 1942.

Jacobs, Stephen W. "California Contemporaries of Frank Lloyd Wright, 1885–1916." In *Problems of the 19th and 20th Centuries,* vol. IV, 34–43. Princeton, NJ: Princeton University Press, 1963.

Jennings, Frederick. "A Theater Designed in the Egyptian Style." *Architect and Engineer* (January 1921): 86–87.

Kouwenhoven, John A. *Half a Truth is Better Than None.* Chicago: University of Chicago Press, 1982.

Lamb, Thomas W. "Some Highlights in Motion Picture Theater Design." *Architect and Engineer* (November 1929): 75-80.

Menten, Theodore. *The Art Deco Style.* New York: Dover Publications, 1972.

Mesic, Julian C. "Today's Apartments." *Architect and Engineer* (December 1930): 29–33.

Moore, Charles, Peter Becker, and Regula Campbell. *The City Observed: Los Angeles.* New York: Vintage, 1984.

Moore, Charles, K. Smith, and Peter Becker, editors. *Home Sweet Home: American Domestic Vernacular Architecture.* Los Angeles: Craft & Folk Art Museum, 1983.

Moore, Patricia Anne. *The Casino: Avalon, Santa Catalina Island, California.* Avalon, CA: Catalina Island Museum Society, 1979.

Morley, Sylvanus G. *The Ancient Maya.* Stanford, CA: Stanford University Press, 1956.

Mumford, Lewis, editor. *Roots of Contemporary American Architecture.* New York: Reinhold Publishing Corporation, 1952.

———. *The Pentagon of Power: The Myth of the Machine.* New York: Harcourt Brace Jovanovich, 1964.

Neely, Jo. "A Dream Come True." *Architect and Engineer* (May 1918): 72–76.

Pichel, Irving. *Modern Theaters.* New York: Harcourt Brace and Company, 1925.

Pildas, Ave. *Art Deco Los Angeles.* New York: Harper & Row, 1979.

Robinson, Cervin and Rosemarie Haag Bletter. *Skyscraper Style.* New York: Oxford University Press, 1975.

Roehrig, Frederick L. "L. A. Power and Light Plants." *Architect and Engineer* (November 1929): 75–80.

Schippers, Donald J. "Walker & Eisen: Twenty Years of Los Angeles Architecture, 1920–1940." *Southern California Quarterly,* vol. XVI, no. 4 (December 1964): 371–394.

Sexton, Randolf Williams. *American Commercial Buildings of Today.* New York: Architecture Book Publishing Company, 1928.

———. *The Logic of Modern Architecture.* New York: Architecture Book Publishing Company, 1929.

Shand, Phillip M. *Modern Picture Houses and Theaters.* Philadelphia: J. B. Lippincott, 1930.

Starr, Kevin. *Material Dreams: Southern California Through the 1920s.* New York: Oxford University Press, 1990.

Whiffen, Marcus. *American Architecture Since 1780: A Guide to the Styles.* Cambridge, MA: MIT Press, 1969

Whiffen, Marcus and Frederick Koeper. *American Architecture 1607–1976.* Cambridge, MA: MIT Press, 1981.

Whitaker, Charles Harris, editor. *Bertram Goodhue: Architect and Master of Many Arts.* New York: Press of the American Institute of Architects, 1925.

White, L. Raymond. "Oil Stations." *Architect and Engineer* (October 1935): 29–35.

Wright, Frank Lloyd. *The Natural House.* New York: Horizon Press, 1954.

94